Builders Jol

The Ultimate Collection of Builders Jokes

By Chester Croker

Jokes for Builders

These jokes for builders will make you giggle. Some of them are old, some of them are current, and while we don't want to plug them too much, we hope you enjoy our collection of the very best building jokes and puns around.

These jokes will prove that builders have a good sense of humor, and you will soon be in stitches and dying with laughter.

I dedicate this book to my dad who was a roofer. So, dad, if you're up there….

Published by Glowworm Press
7 Nuffield Way
Abingdon OX14 1RL

Disclaimer
All rights reserved. No part of this publication may be reproduced in any form or by any means without the written permission of the publisher. The information herein is offered for informational purposes only, and is universal as so. The presentation of the information is without contract or any type of guarantee assurance. Under no circumstances will any legal responsibility or blame be held against the author for any reparation, damages or monetary loss due to the information herein, either directly or indirectly.

FOREWORD

When I was asked to write a foreword to this book I was flattered.

That is until I was told by the author, Chester Croker, that I was the last resort, and that everyone else he had approached had said they couldn't do it!

I have known Chester for a number of years and his ability to create funny jokes is remarkable. He is incredibly quick witted and an expert at crafting clever puns and amusing gags and I feel he is the ideal man to put together a joke book about our much maligned profession.

He will be glad you have bought this book, as he has an expensive lifestyle to maintain.

Enjoy!

Rick Layer

Table of Contents

Chapter 1: Introduction
Chapter 2: One Liner Builder Jokes
Chapter 3: Q&A Builder Jokes
Chapter 4: Shorter Builder Jokes
Chapter 5: Longer Builder Jokes
Chapter 6: Builders Pick-Up Lines
Chapter 7: Bumper Stickers for Builders

Chapter 1: Builders Jokes

If you're looking for funny builder's jokes you've certainly come to the right place.

In this book you will find plenty of builders jokes that will hopefully make you laugh. Some of them are old, but some of them are new, and while we don't want to plug them too much, we hope you enjoy our collection of the very best building jokes and puns around.

We've got some great one-liners to start with, plenty of quick-fire questions and answers themed gags, some story led jokes and as a bonus some cheesy pick-up lines for builders.

This mixture of building jokes will prove that builders have a good sense of humor and they are guaranteed to get you laughing.

Chapter 2: Builder One-Liners

If a builder says he will fix it, he will. There's no need to remind him every six months.

Marble is a valuable building material and should not be taken for granite.

Did you hear about the builder who had too many drinks? He was hammered.

Last week I asked a builder to do some odd jobs for me - I gave him a list of ten jobs, but he only did jobs 1,3,5,7 and 9.

I saw an argument between a carpenter and a hairdresser.

They were going at it hammer and tongs.

Raise your hand if you live in a city whose roads have been under construction since 1000 BC.

I've started this new fad diet. You have to hit garden buildings with a hammer. I'm looking to pound a few sheds.

A book never written – "How to Build a House" by Han D. Mann.

I went to a party with a construction team the other week. They really raised the roof.

Why is a house called a building when it is already built?

I pressed the Hammer function button on my new drill and it keeps playing 'You can't touch this.'

If builders built buildings the way programmers wrote programs, then a woodpecker would be able to destroy most constructions.

I thought about becoming a plumber rather than a builder, but I just couldn't take the plunge.

Why are builders afraid to have a 13th floor but book publishers aren't afraid to have a Chapter 11?

The experienced builder really nailed it, but the new guy screwed everything up.

Did you hear about the lesbian builders who built a timber framed house?

There was not a stud in the place. It was all tongue in groove.

Jesus once said, "He who lives by the sword, will die by the sword." He was a carpenter that died by being nailed to a piece of wood, so he might have had a point.

A builder friend of mine gave me some great advice, saying I should put something away for a rainy day. I've gone for an umbrella.

Before a plumber retires, he takes the final plunge.

Wood you consider lumberjacks to be yew man beings? It's a difficult question, but I have to axe.

Did you hear about the work-shy builder who ran out of sick days so he called in dead.

Builders apprentices are like Christmas lights.

Half of them don't work and the rest aren't very bright.

A team of builders have been at my neighbor's house for a few weeks. The rumor is they're building a library, but it's all been a bit hush-hush.

I rang up a local building firm, and I said, "I want a skip outside my house." He said, "'I'm not stopping you."

When I was younger my most successful chat up line was "Don't sleep with a drip. Call a plumber."

I'd like to build a barn over Christmas, if I can find space in my shed-yule.

The first builder screwed up the job, but the second one really nailed it.

Did you hear about the builder's laborer who stole a calendar?

He got twelve months.

The wife shouted at her builder husband, "Stop staring at bricks. Why can't you just stare at woman like a normal husband?"

I went to a party with some roofers the other week; we let our hair down and we really raised the roof.

A woman in my last job was a builder's wet dream. Flat as a board and easy to nail.

Sign seen on a van: Miller's Builders. We will repair what your husband supposedly fixed.

I once thought about becoming a carpenter, but I didn't think it wood work. Then I thought about being a welder, but I soon realized that steel wooden work.

My wife is a real DIY fan.

Whenever I ask her to do something, she says, "Do it yourself."

I never wanted to believe that my Dad was stealing from his job as a road worker. But when I got home, all the signs were there.

Did you know that Hitler trained to be a carpenter? He even published a book 'Mein Kampfy Chair.' It wasn't successful though - he had a thing against screws.

People call me a builder. Well, I am good at building walls around me.

A plumber is the only person who can take a leak while they fix a leak.

Have you seen the joke that is doing the rounds on various forums about the builder that had to re-do a fence that got messed up? I think it has been re-posted a lot.

Did you hear about the cross-eyed builder who was sacked because he couldn't see eye to eye with his customers.

Did you hear the one about the roofer with a perfect safety record? He never had a shingle accident.

Duct tape is like the force. There is a light side and a dark side and it holds the universe together.

I had to explain what irony was to someone at our church meeting today. Apparently "Being a carpenter and getting nailed to a wooden cross" wasn't a good example.

Porn gives people an unrealistic expectation of how quickly a builder will come to your house.

I got called pretty the other day. Actually, the full sentence was "You're a pretty bad builder." but I'm choosing to focus on the positive.

My local builder refused to make me a kitchen worktop.

He said it would be counter-productive.

I just completed my builders City & Guilds exam. I got B+ for planning, A for sawing and A for hammering. I absolutely nailed it.

I'm going to start a building business that employs illegal immigrants. I'm going to call it Manuel Labor.

Anybody who has any doubt about the ingenuity or the resourcefulness of a builder never got a bill from one.

My apprentice loves driving the steam-roller. He is such a flatterer.

If your hipped roof needs restoration, do you sign up for a hip replacement?

Did you hear the miracle about the blind builder?

He picked up his hammer and saw.

When I was a carpenter, my marriage failed. My wife accused me of being a mahoganist.

The unfortunate builder asked his female customer if she was still mad about the shoddy repair he did last week. She said, "Don't worry; it's water under the fridge."

I think my dog wants to be a roofer. He likes roofing.

Yesterday, a builder's wife asked him to pass her lipstick but he passed her a super-glue stick instead by mistake. She still isn't talking to him.

A builder wanted to buy something for his mother-in-law, so he bought her a new chair. She won't let him plug it in though.

Our apprentice is learning to tap dance.

He isn't very good though - he keeps falling in the sink.

Chapter 3: Question and Answer Builder Jokes

Q: Why did the builder dip his finger in blue ink?

A: *To get a blue print.*

Q: What is the difference between a builder and a surgeon?

A: *When a builder messes something up, they can fix it. But when a surgeon messes something up, they have to bury it.*

Q: Why do builders enjoy fixing steelwork?

A: *Because it's riveting work.*

Q: Who was the first carpenter?

A: *Eve - She made Adam's banana stand.*

Q: How many safety inspectors does it take to change a light bulb?

A: *Four. One to change it and three to hold the ladder.*

Q: Why did the builder's laborer climb onto the roof?

A: *He heard that drinks were on the house.*

Q: What do you call a builder who is happy every Monday morning?

A: *Retired.*

Q: What did the builder do when he got a horny girl into bed with him for the first time?

A: *He screwed, nutted, and bolted.*

Q: How do builders party?

A: *They raise the roof.*

Q: Why is the tasty MILF in the house next door a builder's dream?

A: *She is as flat as a board and easy to nail.*

Q: Why do builders have such large toolboxes?

A: *Because they have to be awl-encompassing.*

Q: Why are lesbians awful carpenters?

A: *They don't know how to handle wood.*

Q: How did the nosy roofer end up doing such a bad job on site?
A: *He couldn't stop eavesdropping.*

Q: What kind of building weighs the least?
A: *A lighthouse.*

Q: How many cowboy builders does it take to change a light bulb?
A: *Three. One to hold the ladder; one to "pretend" to change the light bulb and one to sit in the van.*

Q: How does an Eskimo repair his house?
A: *He uses i-glue.*

Q: Why is Christmas Day like a day at a building site?
A: *You end up doing all the work and some fat guy in a suit takes all the credit.*

Q: Why do bricklayers have trouble getting out of bed in the morning?

A: *Because they are bedded in mortar.*

Q: Why was the builder so short?

A: *Because he had been contracting for a long time.*

Q: Why did the builder's wife leave him?

A: *He was screwing around when he was supposed to be nailing her.*

Q: How many lawyers does it take to roof a house?

A: *It depends on how thinly you slice them.*

Q: Why was the builder's parcel sore?

A: *Because it was a tender package.*

Q. Why do builders laborers' have clear lunch boxes?

A. *So they know whether they are going home or going to work.*

Q: Why did the cannibal builder get disciplined by his boss?

A: *For buttering up his clients.*

Q: What are the only two seasons in the Midwest?
A: *Winter and Construction.*

Q: What are the only two seasons in the South?
A: *Football and Construction.*

Q: Which breakfast gurus would you ask for building advice?
A: *The saw sages.*

Q: How does a builder build a set of stairs?
A: *By thinking one step ahead.*

Q: How did the builder know the board was cut in half?
A: *He saw it.*

Q: What happened when a builder crossed a chili pepper, a shovel and a terrier?

A: *He got a hot-diggity-dog.*

Q: What do you call a woman who is seeing a builder, a plasterer, a plumber, an electrician and a tiler all at the same time?

A: *A jack off all trades.*

Q: Which nails do builders hate hitting?

A: *Their finger nails.*

Q: What does a builder like about carpentry?

A: *He can put his wood where he likes, and get paid for it.*

Q: What is the difference between an ugly woman and a brick?

A: *When you lay a brick it doesn't text you for weeks afterwards.*

Q: What is the most common hospital treatment for roofers?

A: *Hip replacements.*

Q: What do builders and webcam girls have in common?

A: *They both bang their fingers whilst doing their jobs.*

Chapter 4: Short Builder Jokes

I have to admit I'm not a very good builder.

I'm the kind of person that looks at some rolled up pink fiberglass insulation and thinks that it looks like a big piece of sushi.

I only know to call it 'Fiberglass insulation' because I once installed it with a mate who told me that's what it was called.

I was really surprised, that while we were refurbishing a property, he told me that I hammer like lightning.

I was quite pumped until he told me that lightning never hits the same spot twice.

Paddy applies for a job on building site and the foreman asks him if he can drive a forklift, to which Paddy says he can.

The foreman then asks Paddy if he can make tea.

Paddy replies, "How big is the tea pot?"

A builder in my area went to jail for dealing drugs.

I've been one of his customers for over five years, and I had no clue he was a builder.

I went into my local DIY superstore yesterday and asked a member of staff, "Where can I find some hammers, nails, a trowel and a bag of cement?"

The guy replied, "They're all under 'Construction'."

I said, "Where will they be when they're finished?"

Two old builders are talking about sex and one reckons that sex is 75% work and 25% pleasure while the other reckons it's 25% work and 75% pleasure.

They decide to ask their apprentice's opinion to see what he has to say.

"Sex is 100% pleasure," says the apprentice.

"Why do you say that?" ask the builders.

The apprentice replies, "Well, I am the only one working around here."

A builder was caught trading without a license, and his work was considered sub-standard.

In the court the judge received a note from his assistant and immediately declared him guilty for both working without a license and for perjury.

It turned out he had done some jury rigging.

Winters are extremely cold in Minnesota, so the owner of a construction project in the state felt he was doing a good deed when he bought some earmuffs for his foreman.

Noticing, however, that the foreman wasn't wearing the earmuffs even on the bitterest day, the project manager asked, "What's the problem with the muffs I got you?"

The foreman replied, "They're lovely – really warm too."

"Why aren't you wearing them?" the project manager asked.

The foreman explained, "I wore them the day you got them for me, and somebody offered to buy me lunch, but I just didn't hear him. I am not going to risk that happening again."

A hairy dog walks into a bar, and takes a seat and says to the barman, "I would like a large scotch on the rocks please."

The barman is dumbfounded and says, "Well how about that – a talking dog - you should think about joining the circus."

The dog replies, "The circus has a big tent. What would they need a builder for?"

A builder goes into a lumber yard, and asks for some 2 x 4s.

The salesman asks "How long do you want them?" to which the builder replies "Oh, quite a while, I'm going to build a garage with them."

A builder tries to enter an up-market bar, and the bouncer tells him that the door policy means he needs to wear a tie to be allowed in.

The builder knows he has some jump leads in the boot of his car; so he goes and ties these around his neck, and manages to create a passable looking knot too.

He goes back to the bar and the bouncer says: "You can come in now – but just don't start anything."

A builder was re-grouting a bathroom when the lady of the house said to him, "Would it be okay for me to take a bath while you're eating lunch?"

The builder stopped working, sat on the toilet and replied, "It's okay with me lady, as long as you don't splash my sandwiches."

A vicar and a minister were in the vicarage discussing the best positions for prayer while a builder was repairing one of the vicars' kitchen cupboards.

The vicar said, "I find kneeling is the best way to pray."

The minister said, "I get the best results when I am standing with my hands completely outstretched."

The builder told them, "The best praying I ever did was when I was hanging upside down from a ladder."

A doctor hired a builder to do some carpentry work around his house.

The doctor looked over the builder's shoulder as he was applying a piece of molding to cover his uneven cut.

The doctor said, "That's an easy way to hide your mistakes."

The builder replied, "Yes, you're right. I don't need six feet of soil to hide my mistakes."

A builder meets up with his blonde girlfriend as she's picking up her car from the mechanic.

He asks her, "Is everything alright with your car?"

"Yes, thank goodness," the dipsy blonde replies.

The guy asks, "Were you worried that the mechanic might rip you off?"

The blonde replies, "Yes, but he didn't rip me off at all. I was so relieved when he said all I needed to pay for was some blinker fluid."

A woman had a leak in the roof in the dining room, so she called out a builder to take a look at it.

"When did you first notice the leak?" the builder asked her.

"Last night," the woman replied, "when it took me an hour to finish my soup."

A builder tells his doctor that whenever he is at work he gets excessively angry the moment he sees roof tiles, and he loses self-control and starts to break every tile on the roof.

The doctor tells him he suffers from a wreck tile dysfunction.

Gary is doing some roofing.

He nears the top of the ladder and starts shaking and feeling dizzy.

He calls down to his boss and says, "I think I need to go home, I am feeling a little dizzy."

His boss asks, "Do you have vertigo, Gary?"

Gary replies, "No, I live around the corner."

A builder was working on a farm roof when he had the misfortune of falling off and landing in a huge pile of cow manure.

Finding himself up to his neck, he yelled out, "Fire, Fire, Fire."

The local fire department responded quickly, and when they got to the barn, they asked, "Where's the fire?"

"There's no fire," replied the builder as they pulled him out of the pile of dung. "But if I had yelled, 'Sh*t. Sh*t. Sh*t.' who would have come to rescue me?"

Here's one for the kids:- My mate's dog has got a job on a building site - he's a roofer!

While a team of builders were working outside the house I had just bought, I busied myself with indoor cleaning.

I had just finished washing the floor when one of the workmen asked to use the bathroom.

With dismay I looked at his muddy boots and my newly polished floor.

"Just a minute," I said. "I'll put down newspapers."

"That's all right, lady," he responded. "I'm house trained."

The builder grumbled to his friend that his wife didn't satisfy him anymore.

His friend advised he find another woman on the side, pretty quick.

When they met up a month or so later, the builder told his friend, "I took your advice and managed to find a woman on the side, yet my wife still doesn't satisfy me!"

The doorbell rings and the housewife cries out, "Who is it?"

"It's the builder," answers a man from the other side of the door.

She replies, "But we already have a builder working on our roof."

"I know. I just fell off." answered the irate builder.

A builder was talking to two of his buddies about their daughters.

The first friend says, "I was cleaning my daughter's room the other day and I found a pack of cigarettes. I didn't even know she smoked."

The second friend says, "That's nothing. I was cleaning my daughter's room the other day and I found an empty bottle of wine. I didn't even know she drank."

The builder says, "That's nothing. I was cleaning my daughter's room the other day and I found a pack of condoms. I didn't even know she had a penis."

I was chatting to my buddy who is a builder who told me how he had just tiled a huge bathroom and he was very pleased with the result, especially as it was the first time he had taken on a tiling project.

I asked how he learnt how to do it, and he told me that he mostly learned by tile and error.

A builder goes to the doctor with a hearing problem.

The doctor says, "Can you describe the symptoms to me?"

The builder replies, "Yes. Homer is a fat yellow lazy man and his wife Marge is skinny with big blue hair."

A dozy DIY enthusiast takes his front door to his builder friend and says, "Can you fix my front door for me?"

The builder replies, "Sure, but what about your house, what if a burglar was to get in?"

The dozy guy replies, "Impossible. How could he get in when I've got the door right here with me?"

My wife and I once had a lovely weekend away at a village in the countryside.

We became friendly with the local builder who told us that his neighbor had a pretty little cottage for sale.

We went to view the cottage and despite it looking a little neglected, we fell in love with it and bought it.

When we moved in, our builder friend came by to welcome us and said, "You got a great deal, but it does need some work – the plumbing is awful, the wiring is dangerous and the roof leaks."

Dismayed, I said to him, "Why on earth didn't you tell us that before we bought it?" to which he replied, "We weren't neighbors then."

A builder tells his pal he had been working on the roof and that he split his coffee all over the tiles.

He tells his pal that his boss said it was ok though; and that he can wipe the slate clean.

My buddy is not the sharpest tool in the box.

On a job the other day, he was going to use a screw, but I explained to him when to use a screw and when a nail, and for this job I recommended ing nails.

He said to me, "What you're telling me is that I have to strike this thing repeatedly with a hammer?" to which I replied, "Yes, you hit the nail on the head."

A builder is struggling to find a parking space at his local Home Depot.

"Lord," he prayed. "I just cannot cope with this. If you open a space up for me, I promise I'll give up the booze and go to church every Sunday."

All of a sudden, the clouds separated and the sun shone down onto an empty parking space.

Quick as a flash, the builder says, "Never mind Lord, I have managed to find one."

I helped out a builder friend of mine the other day who wanted to lay a new carpet in his den.

We laid out the deep red carpet roll on the lawn so he could measure it properly and cut it to size.

The nosy next door neighbor popped her head over the fence and said if she had any say it, she would prefer it if we kept the lawn its normal color.

A proud father is showing pictures of his three sons to an old work colleague and he is asked, "What do your boys do for a living?"

He replied, "Well my youngest is an attorney and my middle son is a surgeon."

"What does the oldest child do?" his friend asked.

The reply came, "He's the builder that paid for the others' education."

A builder took his cross-eyed Labrador to the vet.

The vet picked the dog up to examine him and said, "Sorry, I'm going to have to put him down."

The builder said, "Oh, it's not that bad is it?"

The vet replied, "No, he's just very heavy."

One winter morning a builder's laborer calls up his boss and says, "I am not coming to work today, I am really sick. I have got toothache, leg ache and stomach ache."

His boss says, "I really need you on the site today. Whenever I feel sick, I go to my wife and have wild passionate sex with her. It instantly makes me feel better and I can go to work. You should try doing that before crying off work."

A couple of hours later the laborer calls his boss again and says, "Boss, I did what you said to do and I feel much better. I will be at work soon. By the way, you've got a lovely house."

A builder was giving evidence in court about an accident that he had witnessed.

The lawyer for the defendant was trying his best to discredit him and he asked the builder just how far away he was from the accident.

The builder replied, "Thirty two feet, nine inches exactly."

The lawyer was stunned and asked, "What? How can you be so sure of that precise distance?"

The builder replied, "Well, I figured that sooner or later some fool would ask me. So, I measured it."

A young boy named John asked his mother if she wanted to play with him.

She said, "No John, but why don't you go next door and watch the builders build that extension."

So, Johnnie goes next door and spends most of the day with the builders as they go about their work.

Later that afternoon he comes into the house, and his mother asks, "John, how was your day with the builders?"

He replies, "Well, first we had to put a goddamn door up, but the motherf*cker didn't fit, so we had to take the cocksucker back down again, shave a few pussy hairs off, and put the piece of shit back up again."

An experienced builder is fixing a roof, when suddenly he slips.

He pushes his strength to the maximum and grabs one of the last tiles he could reach.

He is dangling on the side of the roof and he feels his strength is going, so he yells to his partner, "Tell my wife not to put the lamb on for dinner. I will be eating at the hospital tonight."

A builder was on the top floor of a building and but he had forgotten to bring his saw up with him.

He yells down to his apprentice on the ground floor but the apprentice can't hear him so the builder decides to use sign language.

He points to his eye (I) then his knees (need) then he moves his arms in a sawing motion (saw).

The apprentice nods, pulls down his trousers, and starts to make the motions of wanking.

The builder is furious, rushes down to the lad and yells, "What are you doing? I said I needed a saw."

The apprentice replies, "I know. I was just trying to tell you I was coming."

A builder called Mick calls up his local paper and asks "How much would it cost to put an ad in the paper?"

"Four dollars an inch," the sales woman replies. "What is it that you are selling?"

"A twelve-foot ladder," said Mick before crashing the phone down.

My Uncle Pepe emigrated from Cuba to the US as an adult, and thus had a very hard time dealing with English.

The part he struggled with most was cursing properly.

He worked in construction, and one day one of his worker buddies says, "Man, Pepe, it's hot as a mother*cker."

My Uncle Pepe tried hard to process that, and the next day, trying to fit in, he turns to his buddy and said, "Man, today, it is hot just like when I f*cked your mother."

A builder dies in a car crash on his fortieth birthday and finds himself greeted at the Pearly Gates by a brass band.

Saint Peter comes over, shakes his hand and says, "Congratulations."

The builder asks, "Congratulations for what?"

Saint Peter says, "We are rejoicing that you lived to be 100 years old."

"But that's not the case" says the builder. "I only lived to be forty."

"That's awkward," says Saint Peter, "we have added up your time sheets and your invoices, and the amount you charged you must have reached 100!"

I called my usual builder to complain about my faulty ice making machine that had been leaking.

When he came back out to the house, he discovered it was just some ice that had fallen off the back and melted on the floor.

I apologized and the builder told me not to worry, because as far as he was concerned, it was all water under the fridge.

A builder came home early one day and found his wife in bed with another man.

In his fury he pulled the man out of bed and dragged him downstairs into the garage where he put the man's penis in a vise.

He secured the vise tightly, made sure it was completely shut, and then removed the handle.

He then picked up a junior hacksaw from the tool rack.

The man screamed, "Stop. You're not going to cut my dick off, are you?"

With a grisly gleam of revenge in his eye the builder said, "No. I'm not. You are. I am going to set the garage on fire."

A builder is helping out his roofer buddy Gary for a week.

They are working on a house repairing some roof tiles.

Gary is up on the roof and accidentally cuts off his ear, and he yells down to his friend, "Hey - look out for my ear I just cut off."

The builder looks around and calls up to Gary, "Is this your ear?"

Gary looks down and says "No. Mine had a pencil behind it!"

A burglar has broken into our local Police station and stolen the toilet.

Right now the Police say they have nothing to go on.

Mick and Paddy are working on a building site.

At lunchtime Mick says to Paddy, "I'm going to take the rest of the day off. Watch this. I'm going to pretend I'm mad."

He climbs up the rafters, hangs upside down and yells out, "I'm a light bulb. I'm a light bulb."

The foreman yells, "Mick you're crazy; go home."

So Mick packs up his equipment and leaves the site.

Paddy then begins to pack his stuff up ready to leave as well.

The foreman demands, "What on earth do you think you're doing?"

Paddy replies, "Well, I'm off home too. You can't expect me to work in the dark."

Here is the only knock-knock joke in this book, so here goes:-

Knock, knock.

Who's there?

Ding Dong.

Ding dong who?

Yes, I have fixed your doorbell.

A plasterer, a painter and a bricklayer are arguing whether it better to have a wife or a mistress.

The plasterer says, "It's much better to have a mistress as it involves a high level of excitement."

The painter says, "I reckon it's better to have a wife, as you know here you are, and it's nice and steady – most of the time."

The bricklayer says, "I reckon it's best to have both a wife and a mistress. The wife will think I am with the mistress, and the mistress will think I am with the wife."

An 84 year old retired builder was walking along the road one day when he spotted a frog hopping around.

He reached down, picked it up, and went to put it in his pocket.

As he did, the frog said to him, "Kiss me on the lips and I'll turn into a beautiful woman and make mad crazy passionate love to you."

The old builder ignored this and continued to put the frog in his pocket.

The frog croaked, "Didn't you hear what I said?"

The old builder looked down at the frog and said, "Yes I did, but at my age I'd rather have a talking frog."

The homeowner was delighted with the work the builder had done all around his house.

"You did a great job." he said and handed him his cash.

He then said, "Also, in order to thank you, here's an extra 50 bucks to take the missus out to dinner."

Later that night, the doorbell rang and it was the builder.

The homeowner asked him, "What's the matter, did you forget something?"

"Nope." replied the builder, "I'm just here to take your missus out to dinner like you asked."

A builder had a problem sleeping, and constantly coming into work late, so he went to his doctor, who gave him a pill and told him to take it that night.

The builder slept very well, and actually got up before his alarm went off.

After enjoying a leisurely breakfast, he cheerfully drove to work, where his boss met him on the building site.

"Boss, I think I have got a solution to my sleeping problem," the builder exclaimed.

His boss replied, "That's great, but just where were you yesterday?"

Chapter 5: Longer Builder Jokes

Shingles

A builder walked into a doctor's office and the receptionist asked him what he had.

He replied, "I got shingles."

She said, "Fill out this form with your name, address and medical insurance number. When you're done, please take a seat."

Ten minutes later a nurse's aide came out and asked him what he had.

He said, "I got shingles."

So she took down his height, weight and complete medical history, then said, "Change into this gown and wait for a while in the examining room."

Thirty minutes later a nurse came in and asked him what he had.

He said, "I got shingles."

So she gave him a blood test, a blood pressure test, an electrocardiogram, and told him to wait for the doctor.

An hour later the doctor came in and asked him what he had.

He said, "Shingles."

The doctor gave him a full-cavity examination, and then said, "I just checked you out thoroughly, and I can't find shingles anywhere."

The builder replied, "They're outside in the truck. Where do you want them?"

The Wheelbarrow

A young guy at a building site has annoyed most of the others on the site as he continually brags about how long he spends lifting weights his time in the gym, how strong he is, and how he could out-do anyone on site.

One of the older men decides to teach the gym bunny a lesson.

He says to the younger guy, "Actions speak louder than words. You're a good talker, but let's see you put your money where your mouth is. I'll bet you a week's wages that I can take something over to the other side of this site in a wheelbarrow that you will not be able to wheel back."

The young guy guffaws self-assuredly, "It's a deal old timer. Show me what you've got."

The old guy then takes the wheelbarrow by its handles and then instructs the gym bunny, "Get in the barrow."

Packed Lunch

Three construction workers, an Aussie, a Scot and an Irishman are about to have lunch while sitting on the 30th floor of a construction site.

The Aussie opens his lunch box and groans, "Vegemite again. If my wife makes me another Vegemite sandwich tomorrow, I swear I will jump off this building."

The Scot opens his lunch box and groans, "Och, Haggis again. If I get a haggis sandwich tomorrow, I swear I will jump off this building too."

The Irishman opens his lunch box and groans, "Potato again. I'm sick of potato sandwiches. If I get a potato sandwich again tomorrow, I will jump too."

The next day at lunch the Aussie opens his lunch box to discover another Vegemite sandwich so, true to his word, he jumps. Likewise, the Scot has haggis again, and he also jumps off. The Irishman mournfully eyes another potato sandwich and with a final salute to the world, he jumps off too.

At the funeral a week later, all their wives are gathered together in a circle crying.

The wife of the Aussie says, "Why, oh why, did I only make him Vegemite sandwiches? If only I had changed it at least once, he'd still be alive now."

The Scottish wife says, "Och, I really wish he had told me he wanted a different sandwich filling and he would still be with me now."

The wife of the Irishman looks at the other two women and says, "I don't understand it – the fecking idiot made his own sandwiches."

Three Foreigners

A Spaniard, a Russian and a Korean all worked for the same construction company.

At the start of the day the boss says to the Spanish guy, "You're in charge of the cement."

Then he said to the Russian guy, "You're in charge of the dirt."

Then he said to the Korean guy, "You're in charge of the supplies."

Then he said, "I will be back later to check on your work. It better be good or you're fired."

Tue to his word, at the end of the day, the boss comes back to check on the foreigner's work.

He looks at the big pile of cement and says, "Good work," to the Spanish guy.

He looks at the big pile of dirt and says, "Good work," to the Russian guy.

He couldn't see the Korean guy so he asks, "Where the hell is the Korean guy?"

All of a sudden, the Korean guy jumps out from behind the big pile of dirt and yells, "Supplies."

Job Interview

A construction site boss was interviewing men for a job, when along came Paddy. The boss took an instant dislike to him and thought to himself, "I'm not hiring that lazy guy."

So he decides to set a test for Paddy, hoping he wouldn't be able to answer the questions, and the boss would be able to refuse him the job without getting into an argument.

The first question was, "Without using numbers, represent the number 9."

So Paddy says, "That's easy," and proceeds to draw three tall, leafy trees.

The boss says, "What the hell's that?" Paddy says, "Tree 'n tree n' tree makes nine."

"Fair enough," says the boss. He then says, "Second question, same rules, but this time represent 99."

Paddy stares into space for a while, then makes a smudge on each tree. "There ya go sir," he says.

The boss scratches his head and says, "How on earth do you get that to represent 99?"

Paddy says, "Each tree's dirty now! So it's dirty tree, n' dirty tree n' dirty tree, that's 99."

The boss is getting worried he's going to have to actually hire Paddy, so he decides to up the ante. "Alright, question three. Same rules again, but represent the number 100."

Paddy stares into space again, then he shouts, "Got it!" He makes a little mark at the base of each tree, and says, "There ya go sir, 100."

The boss looks at Paddy's attempt and thinks, 'Ha! got him this time.' Go on Paddy, you must be mad if you think that represents a hundred."

Paddy leans forward and points down to the marks at the tree bases, and says, "A little dog comes along and craps by each tree, see? So now ya gots dirty tree an' a turd, dirty tree an' a turd, an' dirty tree an' a turd, which makes one hundred. When do I start me job?"

The Climbing Frame

A proud father brought home a climbing frame and swing set for his children.

They were excited and were eagerly waiting to play on it.

After an hour of reading the assembly instructions and struggling with trying to fit bolt F into sub-slot G and so on, he gave up and asked an old builder who was working in a neighboring yard to help him.

The old-timer threw the installation instructions away, and he successfully assembled the climbing frame set in under an hour.

The delighted father asked him, "How did you manage to get all that put together successfully without even looking at the instructions?"

"Well, to tell the truth," replied the old-timer, "I can't read, and when you can't read, you've simply got to think."

The Phone Problem

A farmer called his builder buddy to have a look at his weird phone problem – which mostly failed to ring when customers or friends called - and that when it did ring, his dog always howled just before the phone rang.

The builder came to look at the problem and to see if the dog was psychic.

The builder did some tests and found:-

1. The dog was tied to the telephone system's ground wire with a steel chain and collar.
2. The wire connection to the ground earthing rod was loose.
3. The dog received 90 volts of signaling current every time the farm's phone number was called.
4. After a couple of jolts, the dog would start crying and he would then urinate.
5. The wet ground would complete the circuit, thus causing the phone to ring.

The builder thus demonstrated that some problems can be fixed by pissing and crying.

The Young Kid

A building company started construction on an empty lot next to a house owned by a young family.

The young family's five year-old daughter took an interest in what was going on next door and began talking with the workers.

They loved having her around, and they let her sit with them while they had their tea breaks, and they gave her a little job here and there to make her feel useful.

At the end of the week the foreman gave her a pay envelope containing fifteen dollars to thank her.

The little girl took the money home to her mother who suggested that they go to the bank and open a savings account.

When they got to the bank the teller asked the little girl how she had got her own pay check at such a young age.

The little girl proudly replied, "I worked this week with a construction crew who are building a new house next to mine."

"That's very interesting," said the teller, "and do you think you will work on the new house next week as well?"

The young girl replied, "I will do if those useless son of-bitches at the builder's merchants ever deliver the f*cking drywall."

Train Passengers

A builder, a lawyer, a beautiful lady, and an old woman were on a train, sitting 2x2 facing each other.

The train went into a tunnel and when the carriage went completely dark, a loud "smack" was heard.

When the train came out of the tunnel back into the light the lawyer had a red hand print on his face. He had been slapped on the face.

The old lady thought, "That lawyer must have groped the young lady in the dark and she slapped him."

The hottie thought, "That lawyer must have tried to grope me, got the old lady by mistake, and she slapped him."

The lawyer thought, "That builder must have groped the hottie, she thought it was me, and slapped me."

The builder sat there thinking, "I can't wait for another tunnel so I can slap that lawyer again!"

Golf With A Priest

A builder was playing a round of golf with his priest and the builder was having a bad round.

On the first hole he swung his club and missed the ball.

He yelled, "God damn it, I missed."

The priest rebuked him saying, "You shouldn't curse, or God may punish you."

The builder waved him off, swung again, missed the ball again and once again he shouted out, "God damn it, I missed."

The priest exclaims, "Thou shalt not take the name of thy Lord in vain. Be warned, the Lord might strike you down with lightning for taking his name in vain."

The builder laughed him off, swung a third time, missed the ball once more, and yet again the builder yelled out, "God damn it, I missed."

Before the priest could say anything, an ominous dark cloud appeared and all of a sudden a ferocious lightning bolt came down hitting the priest, killing him instantly.

A thunderous deep voice was then heard from above saying, "God damn it, I missed."

A Big Complainer

Last week I came home from a hard day at work, only to be moaned at by my wife. She says that the stairs are creaking and that I should fix it.

I tell her, "Do I look like a builder?" and she walks out of the room.

The next day I get home from an exhausting day at work and my wife is moaning again, this time telling me the toilet doesn't flush anymore.

I say, "Do I look like a plumber?" and she leaves me in peace.

The next day I get home from a long day at work and she is moaning again. She says the walls in the main room are looking tired, and need painting.

I tell her, "Do I look like a painter?" and she walks away.

The next day I come home from work late, and I notice the stairs have been fixed, the toilet flushes and the walls have been freshly painted.

I say, "How did this happen?"

She said the baker down the road had done it all.

I say, "How much did it cost?"

She said she could have either baked him a cake, or given him a good time.

I asked her, "What kind of cake did you bake?"

She then said to me, "Do I look like a baker?"

Bar Chat

A young bricklayer is sitting down at the bar having a drink after a hard day's graft, when a large, burly sweaty construction worker sits down next to him.

They start to talk and have a few beers together.

In due course they begin to chat about the prospect of nuclear war.

The builder asks the construction worker, "If you heard the sirens go off, and you knew that the nuclear missiles were on their way, and you know you've twenty minutes or so left to live, what would you do?"

The construction worker replies, "I am going to grab anything that moves and enjoy some quick and dirty sex."

The construction worker then asks the bricklayer what he would do to which he replies, "I'm going to keep perfectly still."

The Sexy Housewife

A builder was called out to repair a squeaky door.

The woman who called him was incredibly sexy and very flirtatious as the builder went about his work.

After he had finished she paid him and said, "I'm going to make a request to you. It's embarrassing to talk about, but while my husband is a kind, decent man - sigh - he has a certain physical weakness. Now, I'm a woman and you're a strong man."

The builder was finding it hard to control himself.

He said, "Yes, I am sure I am able to help you out. What exactly would you like me to do?"

She said, "Well, I've been itching to ask you ever since you came through the door."

The builder quivered, "Yes, Yes. What would you like me to do?"

The woman then asked, "Would you please help me move the refrigerator?"

The Mynah Bird

A builder is making some repairs to the outside of a small house, when the owner, a frail old lady, invites him inside a cup of tea and a slice of cake.

In the kitchen there is an agitated Doberman salivating and gently growling, and in a huge cage on the worktop is a mynah bird chirping away cheerfully.

The lady excuses herself, and the builder asks if he will be safe in the room with the dog to which she replies, "My dog Frankie wouldn't hurt a fly." But then she adds, "Oh. But whatever you do, do NOT say anything to my mynah bird."

As soon as the old lady leaves, the mynah bird starts making a terrible din and starts calling the builder all kinds of rude names.

The builder just glares at the bird and commands, "Just be quiet, you stupid squawk box."

The bird is taken aback and goes very quiet, and a few seconds later, it screeches, "Stick it to him, Frankie."

Take Two

A young boy was watching a builder working on the upper storey of a house. He watched the builder drop a hammer, and saw him climb down the ladder to retrieve it.

The boy tells him, "My daddy would have two hammers so he wouldn't have to climb down the ladder when he dropped one."

The builder climbs back up the ladder and returns to work.

Within a few minutes, he drops his screwdriver, and climbs back down the ladder.

The boy tells him, "My daddy would have two screwdrivers so he wouldn't have to climb down the ladder when he dropped one."

A little while later, the builder has to go to the bathroom.

Unfortunately, he has no way of getting inside the house, so he climbs down the ladder and relieves himself behind a bush.

As he is finishing up, he notices that the little boy has followed him and is watching him, so he asked the lad, "Well, I suppose your daddy has two of these too?"

"No," says the boy, "but my daddy's is twice as big."

Train Noise

A couple live very close to train tracks and the trains make a rattling noise whenever they pass. They have to sleep with ear plugs in the noise is so loud and irritating.

Whenever a train passed, the closet door next to the bedroom would wobble in its sliders to add to the noise.

One day, when her husband was at work, the wife decided to call in a builder to tray and fix it.

He was there within the hour and he witnessed the effect when a train passes, but he wasn't sure what caused the door to wobble or what he needed to do to sort it out.

He decided to sit inside the closet and wait for the next train to pass, so that he could see what was causing the problem.

He took off his tool belt and left it outside the closet, and went inside.

While he was inside the closet, the husband happened to come home early.

He goes upstairs to change out of his work clothes, and he is really angry when he sees the builder's boots in front of the bedroom, and his tool belt next to the closet.

He opens the closet to find the builder and he demands, "Are you having an affair with my wife? What the hell are you doing in my closet?"

The builder replies, "You won't believe this Mister, but I'm waiting for a train."

The Old Man

A passer-by comes across an old man who is crying his eyes out, and he asks him what the problem is.

"Well," says the old chap, "For a long time, I was a builder and employed a few guys, and I sold my building business a few years ago for a tidy sum."

The passer-by says, "So what's up?"

The old man moans, "I own a large house."

The passer-by says, "So what's up?"

The old man wails, "I own a lovely car."

The passer-by says, "So tell me what's up?"

The old man weeps, "A couple of months I married a really young super sexy glamour model."

The passer-by says, "Lucky you - so what exactly is the problem?"

The old man sniffles mournfully, "I can't remember where I live."

The Lawyer

Arriving home after a late night at the office, a lawyer at a prominent law firm found out that his basement was completely flooded. He phoned a builder to get the problem solved.

The builder told the lawyer to turn off the stop cock, and he arrived within the hour, wearing a baseball cap that said 'Blue Collar Guy.'

The builder went down into the basement to investigate the flooding.

Before long, the builder came back upstairs and said, "I have fixed the problem and I'm almost finished. I'm going to write up your bill, and then I'm going to get a part I need to finish the job from my van."

The builder added, "The cap that you mentioned, it's because I'm looking for a new assistant, and I thought you might know somebody who wanted the job."

The lawyer arrogantly replied, "I'm a hot-shot lawyer. Why would I know anyone who would want to work as a builder's mate?"

The builder merely shrugged his shoulders, handed the lawyer his bill, and went to his van.

A few minutes later, after the builder returned from his van, the lawyer said, "I looked over your bill while you were in your van. You have found yourself a new assistant!"

The Broken Leg

An old builder shuffles down the road with his leg in a cast when he meets an old friend.

His friend asks, "How did you break your leg?"

The builder replied, "A customer of mine had promised his wife that he would fix the sink on a particular day. That day, he knew he would need to have to stay late at work, so he called me to sort it out. I went to the man's office to get the house key, and then I went to his house and got to work."

He continued, "When the wife got home, she saw my bottom half sticking out from underneath the sink. She must have assumed I was her husband, and she proceeded to remove my trousers and give me some intimate attention, if you know what I mean."

Then her phone rang, and the woman stopped doing what she was doing to answer it. When she returned, she angrily said, "That was my husband on the phone, so who the hell are YOU?"

The builder continued, "When I got up to speak to her, I bumped my head and knocked myself out. The woman must have pulled me out, fastened my trousers and then called an ambulance."

"When the medics were carrying me out, they asked me what had happened. When I told them, they laughed so much that they dropped me. That's when I broke my leg."

Three Friends

Ron is chatting to his pals, Jim and Shamus.

Jim says, "I think my wife is having an affair with a builder. The other day I came home and found a spirit level under our bed and it wasn't mine."

Shamus then confides, "Well I think my wife is having an affair with an electrician. The other day I found wire cutters under the bed and they weren't mine."

Ron thinks for a minute and then says, "Well I think my wife is having an affair with a horse."

Both Jim and Shamus look at him in disbelief.

Ron sees them looking at him and says, "No, seriously. The other day I came home early and found a jockey under our bed."

Master Van Echo

Back in the Middle Ages there was a man named Poly Van Echo who worked as a builder. He spent years honing his craft, working under many master builders until one day he rose to prominence and became the official builder to the King.

A couple of years later, the King came to him after a heavy rainstorm, and said, "Master Van Echo, the rain has caused all the bridges in our kingdom to rot. Citizens are unable to go to market; farmers cannot bring their crops forth to sell, under risk of a collapse. Can you do something?"

Poly went to work immediately rebuilding the bridges.

It took many weeks, but finally all the wooden bridges in the kingdom were rebuilt, stronger than ever.

He came to the palace and said "My liege, the work is complete."

The King replied "Yes, the bridges are rebuilt, but what if the rains were to come again? Will they not give way to rot again?"

The builder shook his head and said, "No your highness, for I have developed a special compound that promises to keep our bridges free of rot. Just see how they glimmer in the sun with renewed strength against the rain."

The King nodded his approval and called his closest advisers to confer.

After a few minutes he announced, "Master Van Echo, for your service to the kingdom, we grant you land and title."

"Yes Poly, you're a Thane."

A Genie In The Lamp

A builder finds a genie in a lamp, and the genie tells him, "I can only grant you just one wish. What is it that you would like?"

The builder responds, "Carpentry is my passion so I would love to be able to talk to my tools. They are my friends, after all."

The genie says, "Your wish is my command."

Later that day, the builder is working on the frame of a house when he picks up his hammer.

The builder says to the hammer, "Well, I can now talk to my tools. What would you like to say?"

The hammer replies, "I'm hammer."

"Yes, I know that" says the builder. "Is that it?"

"I'm hammer" says the hammer.

The builder is frustrated and turns to his trusty wrench.

The builder says, "What about you? What can you say?"

"I'm wrench", says the wrench.

The builder is annoyed, and he asks his saw, spirit level, screw driver and trowel the same questions, only to hear, "I'm saw, I'm spirit level, I'm screw driver, I'm trowel and so on."

The builder gives up for the day. He drives home, frustrated but believing he will be able to forget all about his wish and relax in front of the TV. He gets home and sees a plank of wood next to the sofa.

"What is going on?" exclaims the builder to which he gets the reply "I'm bored."

Which Nails?

Two builders were working on a house, an experienced guy and one new to the job. The young one, who was nailing down siding, would reach into his nail pouch, pull out a nail and either toss it over his shoulder or nail it in.

The older one asked, "Why are you wasting those perfectly good nails?"

The younger of the two explained, "If I pull a nail out of my pouch and it's pointed toward me, I throw it away because it's defective. If it's pointed toward the house, then I nail it in."

"You idiot," the older builder exclaimed. "The nails pointed toward you aren't defective. Those nails are for the other side of the house."

Reunion

A group of builders, all aged 40, discussed where they should meet for lunch. They agreed to meet at a place called The Smokehouse Grill because the barmaids had big breasts and wore short-skirts.

Ten years later, at age 50, they once again discussed where they should meet for lunch.

It was agreed that they would meet at The Smokehouse Grill because the food and service was good and there was an excellent beer selection.

Ten years later, at age 60, the builders again discussed where they should meet for lunch.

It was agreed that they would meet at The Smokehouse Grill because there were plenty of parking spaces, they could dine in peace and quiet, and it was good value for money.

Ten years later, at age 70, the friends discussed where they should meet for lunch.

It was agreed that they would meet at The Smokehouse Grill because the restaurant was wheelchair accessible and had a toilet for the disabled.

Ten years later, at age 80, the retired builders discussed where they should meet for lunch.

Finally it was agreed that they would meet at The Smokehouse Grill because they had never been there before.

Brown Paper Larry

A cowboy rides into a strange town and sees a builder applying some finishing touches to a gallows so he asks, "Hey, is there going to be hanging?"

The builder nods and says,"Yep. We're fixing up the gallows so they can hang Brown Paper Larry."

The cowboy asks, "How come he's called Brown Paper Larry?"

"Well," says the builder, "Larry always wears clothes that are made from brown paper. Brown paper shirts. Brown paper pants. Even brown paper socks."

The cowboy contemplates this for a moment, then asks, "What are they hanging him for?"

The builder replies, "Rustling."

On God Making Woman

And God Created Woman.

He was so pleased with his creation that he calls in three of his top advisers: His chief builder, His chief tailor, and His chief architect. He presents his creation to them and asks for their suggestions and comments.

The builder said, "There are too many forms, you need to straighten things out, flatten it out."

God replies, "Thank you for your comments, but I like it that way."

The tailor said, "There are too many strings (hair) sticking out, you need to trim them."

God replies, "Thank you for your comments, but I like it that way."

The architect said, "Wonderful creation, absolutely superb, but next time, please don't put the toilets next to the reception room."

Pulling Power

Carlo the property developer and his builder buddy John, went bar-hopping every week together, and almost every week Carlo would pull a hot woman while John went home alone.

One week John asked Carlo his secret to picking up women. "That's easy," said Carlo "When she asks you what you do for a living, don't tell her you're a builder. Tell her you're a lawyer."

Later John is dancing with a hot woman when she leans in and asks him what he does for a living.

"I'm a lawyer," says John. The woman smiles and asks, "Want to go back to my place? It's just around the corner."

So, they go to her place, have some fun and an hour later, John is back in the bar telling Carlo about his success.

"I've only been a lawyer for an hour," John tittered, "And I've already screwed someone!"

Manure

Two builders were putting a new roof on a remote farm barn and they had just about finished for the day when a bundle of shingles slid down the slope and knocked their ladder over.

As they knew no-one would hear them shout, they decided to take drastic measures to get down off the building.

On one side of the barn was a big soft manure pile, and the younger of the two builders decided to jump first, and let the pile of manure break his fall.

After hearing a squishy landing the older builder shouted, "How deep did you go?" to which the younger builder roofer replied, "I went up to my ankles."

So the second builder jumps off the building into the pile of manure, but he sinks down with manure all the way up to his neck.

He yells at his junior, "I thought you said you went up to your ankles."

His junior replied, "I did, but I landed head first."

A Murder Scene

A workman was killed at a construction site, and the police started questioning the suspects.

The electrician was suspected of wiretapping in the past, but he was never charged.

The painter had a brush with the law several years ago.

The glazier went to great panes to conceal his past. He still claims that he was framed.

The carpenter thought he was a stud. He had tried to frame another man several years ago.

The builder claimed he was high at the time.

The police arrested the builder, as the evidence against him was irrefutable, because it was found that the workman, when he died, was hammered.

Suspicious Minds

A builder suspects his wife is having an affair, so he calls her and asks her where she is.

"I'm at home, making dinner, darling." she replies.

"Turn on the blender that so I can hear it," commands the builder.

The wife duly turns on the blender and the builder hears it noisily whirring around.

The next day the builder comes home early from work to find his son alone in the kitchen.

He asks his son, "Where is your mother?"

"I don't know," answered the son, "she went out somewhere with the food blender."

Three Wishes

An owner of a building company and two of his crew are busy digging foundations for a house extension when they come across an old, tarnished brass lamp.

Sure enough, after rubbing the lamp, a genie comes out and grants them three wishes, one for each of them.

The first laborer eagerly says, "I would like to go to Barbados and have an endless supply of cold beer and be left there forever."

The genie grants him his wish and with a puff of smoke and a flash of light, the junior roofer is gone.

The second laborer then says, "I'd like to spend the rest of my life in a villa in Thailand, surrounded by beautiful women that worship me."

The genie also grants him his wish and with another puff of smoke and a flash of light, he is gone too.

The genie turns to the boss and says, "What would you like?" to which he replies with a grin, "Let me take my lunch break and then I want those two back digging on this site."

Chapter 6: Builders Pick-Up Lines

I don't just lay bricks.

I hope you don't mind a bit of banging.

If you're looking for someone who can be in and out in no time at all, then I'm your man.

Do you want to find out why they call me "Enormous Bill"?

I will be twice the size of your estimate.

Wanna play carpenter? First we get hammered, then I'll nail you.

Your eyes are like wrenches - they make my nuts tighten.

You look like you could use a good plunging.

Is there anything you'd like me to screw?

I know how to use my equipment.

Want to see my tool?

I want to nail you.

I will show you what a real stud is.

Want to play Pinocchio? I'll sit on your face and you can tell me lies.

You turn my two-by-four into a four-by-eight.

I can use my snake to clean out your pipes.

I can hammer all day long.

Your eyes are like wrenches. They make my nuts tighten.

If there's anything I know how to do the right way, it's lay pipe.

I'm very good at tongue-and-groove work.

Are you a sucker for a man who knows how to use his equipment?

Can I show you my plumbers crack?

I always wear protection.

I will make it last a long time.

Want to flux?

Let's play carpentry. First we get hammered, I get some wood and then I nail you.

Can I tinker with your pipes?

Is there anything you'd like me to screw?

I always wear my hard hat, baby.

I am a professional pipe layer.

I've got wood – permanently.

Want to see my plunger?

Chapter 7: Bumper Stickers for Builders

There's no such thing as too many tools.

I'd rather be pouring concrete.

Real men play in the dirt.

Sawdust is man glitter.

If a builder can't fix it, then no one can.

Keep Calm and call a builder.

Eat, Sleep, Fix Stuff.

I'm here because you broke something.

My inspiration is a Jewish carpenter from a long time ago.

Real men become builders.

Call a builder. We'll repair what your husband messed up.

Have no fear. The builder is here.

I'd rather be building.

If you think it's expensive hiring a good builder; just try hiring a bad one.

Chapter 8: Summary

Hey, that's pretty well it for this book. I hope you've enjoyed it.

I've written a few other joke books for other professions, and here are just a few sample jokes from my plumbers joke book:-

Q: Why did the plumber retire early?
A: *He was flushed with success.*

Q: What kind of dreams does a plumber have?
A: *Pipe dreams.*

Q: What is a plumber's least favorite vegetable?
A: *A leek.*

Q: Why was the plumber depressed?
A: *His career went down the toilet.*

About The Author

Chester Croker, known to his friends as Chester the Jester, has written many joke books, and has twice been named Comedy Writer of the Year by the International Jokers Guild.

One of his first ever jobs was as a bricklayer's apprentice, and he has come across many interesting characters in the building industry in his life, which provided him with plenty of material for this joke book. Chester is known to his friends as either Chester the Jester or Croker the Joker!

I hope you enjoyed this collection of builders jokes and I hope they brought a smile to your face.

If you see anything wrong in this book, or have a gag you would like to see included in the next version of the book, please visit the glowwormpress.com website.

If you did enjoy the book, kindly leave a review on Amazon so that other builders can have a good laugh too.

Thanks in advance.

Printed in Great Britain
by Amazon